purple
sunset

noor sclafani

noor sclafani purple sunset

2019

www.bookbaby.com

to mom and ben

this book includes a collection of poetry and prose that was written over the span of approximately 15 years. the writings cover a wide range of topics related to life, such as love, friendship, childhood, healing, growth, rejection, nature, pain and sorrow, and illness and death. i thank my husband and friend, farhiya, for encouraging me to create this book.

to ground and to uplift.

contents

purple sunset

the day was long
and hard
filled with mixed emotions
and different experiences
some painful
and some pleasant.
what is this life?
why do i live it?
and what does it mean to me?
i rubbed my eyes
and held my heart.
then i turned toward the ocean
for inspiration.
i found my mind
riding the waves.
and on the horizon,
i saw the day melting away
and the colors of the day
and night converging,
showing me
the mystery and beauty
of life
come together
in a purple sunset.

a thousand

i've laughed a thousand suns.
i've cried a thousand oceans.
i've smiled a thousand moons.
i've loved a thousand flowers.
i've wished a thousand stars.
i've hoped a thousand petals.
i've feared a thousand storms.
i've dreamt a thousand nights.
i've mourned a thousand winters.
i've survived a thousand times.

whispers

your heart
always whispers.
be in silence more
so that you may listen to it.

Life said

Life said,
you think i'm tearing you apart.
what i'm tearing are fallacies about me.
i am the calm
but i am also the storm.
i will storm through your heart.
i will storm through your mind.
and i will shake the ground beneath you.
but i will also give you beauty, serenity, and love.
the scenic landscapes
that you admire and paint on your canvas
were created with passion
and fierceness by me.
and soon you will realize and see
that i was never tearing you apart.
i was turning you into a stunning. work. of. art.

whole

i won't promise you
another half.
i will promise you
that you came into this world
complete
and whole.

dust to star

the path to enlightenment is experience.
you will start as dust
mature to a star
and end as a supernova.
this is your destiny.

the well

my love for you
is like a well
that deepens inside
of me over time.
it has no bottom
just abundance.

the heart

the heart is a sacred place.
it houses your secrets
desires
dreams
distress
and despair.
it's a temple
and a bridge between your spirit
and the heavens.
it's your life's engine
flooding your veins with love
and animating you with energy.
behold the beauty
of your heart.

before and after

she has seen birth
and she has seen death.
she has seen health
and she has seen illness.
she has lived before
and after all four.

inner light

there's no greater guide
than your inner light.
you may not know it
but it burns day and night.
the light is your greatest might.
unite with your light.

canaries

the most joyful experience in life
comes from opening our hearts
and sharing what's in them.
it's a type of freedom
that makes our spirits leap.
it's like freeing beautiful canaries
from their cages.
they begin to sing.
the most painful experience
is shutting our hearts
because what we've shared
has been taken for granted.
the door to the heart
is heavy and flings open with joy
but is difficult and painful to close.
and you can't always bring all the canaries back.
you may have to nurture new ones.

beloved

one can look in the mirror
and wipe the tears from the eyes
but only the beloved
can wipe the tears that the heart cries.

bandages

sometimes we must peel off our bandages
no matter how thick we've layered them.
expose the wounds that we've been covering for years
no matter how painful the exposure may be
as the air hits the wounds
and the exposure does not spare our hearts or vision.
we must clean the wounds
no matter how sharp the sting may be
and tend and nurture them
because they are wounds that we can fully feel and see.
the weight of wounds
can be like an anchor tied to our spirits.
to heal and grow
we must treat our wounds to move forward in life.
not all that heal will fully disappear
and some will still cause aches here and there.
however, they will remain a reminder
that we have lived and survived.

woman

you have kissed the rose
that has stung your lips
yet the taste is as sweet as honey.
the beauty of a gazelle
and the flight of a bat
but as she sits there, she's a dove.
princes have fought
blood has been lost
yet she continues to give life
and holds her heir in her arms.
elusive yet so absolute.
mesmerizing and astute.
follow her; she is your teacher.
she speaks, even without words
listen to the unheard.
poetry has been written
souls have been smitten
as she places flowers on the table.
the queen of spades.
she will get to your heart
and suddenly you've fallen in love.
she is marvelous
your best companion
the listener, the guide
the flaming sun, your closest star.
she is woman.

fragment of eternity

fear not for your life…
you are
a fragment of eternity.
your soul
is the fragrance of the eternal rose.
your body
is the vision of the eternal artist.
your mind
is a page from the book of eternity.
your face
is an image in the mirror of eternity.
your heart
is a beat from the eternal drum.
and your death
is the opening of the eternal door.

inner child

oftentimes we forget
the inner child in us
and perhaps that the inner child
needs to be loved and embraced.
there's a chance
that we abandoned
that inner child
along with its
feelings, desires, and fears
a long time ago.
once we learn to cradle
our inner child
we will find ourselves
and become
who we were always meant to be
which is
one with our inner child.
that inner child is truly us
and to be free
we must set our inner child free.

affinity

there are some
who you meet.
destiny.
undone becomes done.
for a minute
absolute clarity
like the look in their eyes
you see your reflection
watching you.
compelling
to yourself
of yourself.
affinity
in closeness and proximity.
you forget everything
and you just can't figure out
whether they've stepped into you
or you've stepped into them.

the path

it seems like you struggle with your path.
you want a straight path
but your path has turns.
you only have one path.
you're going to have to walk it.

stars

sometimes focusing
on the brightness of others
makes us forget that
we, too, are stars.

rejection

rejection has caused many wounds
broken many hearts
and shattered many dreams.
people have cried rivers
and have drowned in the tragedy of rejection
but it has also made many grow.
the deeper you are thrown
into the earth
the stronger you must be to rise.
rejection is a growing pain
one that exposes us to ourselves
and makes us
reach for something new.
it shows us our humility
and shows us our might.
it helps us overcome all that
we thought we should have achieved
and all that we have failed.
one comes to learn
that rejection is a tough guide
that points to a better direction.
a failed dream
can lead to a fulfilling reality.

clairvoyance

sometimes you can see
events happening
before they happen.
it's as if
life is preparing you
for what's ahead.
it's our third eye.
it's our sixth sense.
it's clairvoyance.

crooked

we are all crooked.
why try to be straight?
why discriminate against
the sick one
who didn't do anything to you?
you fear what you don't know
until it comes your way
and the doctor tells you, stage late.
you want to show
that there's more to you
than a disease.
it's unsettling
taking away all
that you thought you had
but now you have
an ailing body
that nobody wanted.
you want to overcome
yet it takes you down
like a child needing to be cradled
not yet in the tomb
but again
in the nourishment of the womb.
rise from the wounds
those world-inflicted
and those self-inflicted.

twins

hurt and anger
are twins.
you can't tend to your hurt
if you don't address
your anger.

seasons

the beauty of the seasons
doesn't cease to amaze us.
each year
we experience the repeated seasons
with awe and inspiration.
experience your own seasons
with even more wonder
since each of them
will only come once in your lifetime.

i said

i said, "Life
you cut me
and you owe me
some heart beats
that i've missed.
tears have filled
the gaps in my heart.
now give me
what i've wished."
then Life said,
"i gave you
the gift of depth
and opened your heart
to increase your capacity
to love
and so you may receive
understanding
that you'll impart."

let go

we don't make sense anymore.
our vibe doesn't jibe.
please let me go.
don't try to hold
my slipping hand any tighter.
i want to fly higher.
let go
and let's go
in different directions
create a course correction.
let's pass one another
in this soirée of life.
there are other things to do
and to get to
for me and for you.
let go.

road

it's a long
and broken road
but i promise
you'll see
flowers
and other beautiful things
along the way
which will make
the journey
worthwhile.

roots

let the pain out
so the joy can come in.
let the tears clear the way
for happiness to arrive.
the soul that bares the heaviness of grief
is the soul that can be propelled into felicity.
the lungs that have cried hard
are the lungs that will laugh harder.
the ones who have borne frowns in difficulty
are the ones who will smile in simplicity.
the rebound after tragedy will be long
but resilience will build.
after every fall
you will stand again.
you will grow strong
roots going into the ground.

come again

my eyes open the way the flower opens
and looks up at the sun.
and behind my eyes
is the conscious sun of infinite creation.
i am a flower
in the flowerbed of infinity.
i will die every winter
and will be born every spring
from the spring of infinity.
the way the ocean evaporates
and becomes a cloud
i will be lifted into the sky
and i will come back down again
and again.

the slingshot

when you feel set back in life
imagine yourself in a slingshot
getting ready to be propelled
further in life.
sometimes we must feel a pullback
in order to push
ourselves further
to find that drive in us
to find ourselves
and what we want.

children

you may plant them
but they are the flowers of tomorrow.
you have planted the seeds
and they are only yours to sow
so that they may bloom.
do not water them too much
or deny them of the sun
or even the wind and the storm
as they need fury to grow strong.
they were brought by you
not bought by you.
you carry them and hold them.
do not hold on so long
so that they cannot run on their own
or fly to reach their prime.
you love them.
they love you.
but they should not be
a prisoner of your love.
instead a boomerang
that you throw into the sky
that keeps returning to you
time and time again.
a prisoner desires
only to escape and never return.

dirt

we recoil
at the thought of struggle.
we forget
that a flower blooms
from a plant
that emerges
from a seed
that is planted
in dirt.
that's how
it meets the sun.

the savage

you who think you're above animals
are a savage nonetheless.
you have pillaged and stolen
the homes of many.
you have a false sense of entitlement
and have made this world your slave
and you ponder what species
has wit close to yours.
you have slaughtered, eaten, and wasted
and you think you're more skilled and adept
than your prey.
you don't realize that what you've wasted
will be taken by the vulture or the insect
which is smaller than you.
your hubris is so blinding that
you forget that the germs you cannot see
can take the life out of you.
you have an insatiable appetite.
all you do is take from the earth
and instead of giving back in equity
you only give your weak and feeble self
to the grave.
ignorance and arrogance is your name.
you forget
that you are above the earth
for a limited period
and that one day the earth will eat you, too.

mama

i knew her
without anyone telling me who she was.
her love created a bond between us
that cultivated my being
developed my heart
and extended my arms
so that i may reach her hands to hold onto
to stand, and then to walk
wobbly, and then on my own.
i call her mama.

fear

sometimes we try to push fear out
the minute it gets its foot in the door.
but we must let the uncomfortable fear in
and give it the most comfortable seat in our lives
because it can teach us
some of the deepest secrets of our hearts.

love

love brings a smile to my heart and tears to my eyes.
it has both crushed my soul and lifted my spirit to heights i never
knew existed.
it has centered my life, and it has brought chaos.
love locked me and unlocked me.

when i love, i think i've reached love's summit, but love proves me wrong
every time.
it grabs me by the hand and has me dancing to the point where i fall to
my knees.
it manages to pick me up again.
love is so proud; it wins every time and keeps me going.

...to love is to endure, time and time again...
it is the rough and deep Atlantic that meets the waiting coast and creates
a cool breeze.
it is the moon that you can't see above the clouds, but you know is there,
even during the darkest night.
it is the sun that rises when the darkest night has ended.
it is the prick that you feel when you pick a rose.
the rose looks at you and says, "i am beautiful, but i am also mighty. are
you, too?"

i've loved so much that i am in poverty and have become love's beggar.
i have also attained its riches to the point where i am royalty above the
world's kingdoms.
i am both a queen and a beggar before love.
love asks me, "how do you do?" i respond, "i love."

man

he has the eye of an eagle
the mind of a lake
and the heart of the earth.
he works day and night
making tools
and guiding lost souls to shelter.
his arm is a wing
when lifted it shows his might
and under it you will find comfort.
he has the warmth of a summer night
and the calmness of a lullaby.
he connects the world like a constellation
yet he can be reckless
like a child playing with a rock
who hits his friend in the eye
and then cries
at odds
but never against anyone.
his life consists of sacrifice and pride.
he is the greatest paradox.
a magnet. a settling force.
an architect. a paragon.
he is man.

hurt mind

you laugh and say, that person is crazy
but you've never looked in a mirror on the wall
to find yourself staring at a shattered image.
each piece is a part of the past
stitched together in that person's mind.
they wish they could see themselves clearly
for who they are.
regain a time that they could claim as their own
but now their days are filled
with the broken fragments of yesterday.
they need the gentleness of a lamb
and the guidance of a shepherd
but they remain behind closed doors.
a hostage of their mind
afraid to let anyone in or let themselves out.

change

just because people
say they've changed
doesn't mean
that their change
will change your heart.

nature

to be with nature
is to be with yourself.
to experience nature's beauty
is to experience the beauty within you.
as you walk through the valley outside
you walk through the valley within.
as you walk through the field of flowers
you walk through the field of flowers in you.
the feeling that beauty in nature provides you
already belongs to you.
that beauty would not be recognized
if that beauty did not already exist in you.
nature is of you and you are of nature
you are a continuum of it, and it is a continuum of you.
and everything about it
is written in the fabric of your creation.

friendship

if the world had a spirit
i'd say that spirit's name is friendship.
ask of it or not, it is there.
friendship is neither bashful nor bold
but it meets us the way a finger meets the string of a harp.
when the harp is played
there's a known and unknown comfort
going out in waves through the universe.
it is sincere and naked
like a sheep that's been sheared for relief from the summer's heat.
it is where two thirsty individuals meet to drink out of the same river.
one fills a cup and gives it to the other to drink.
the other refills the cup and gives it back for the first to drink.
they remain in this exchange to quench each other's thirst.
it is neither competitive nor vain, but open
like a door that does not even need to be there.
it is so resilient
that the wind may break one of its branches
but the friends' roots will continue to grow
so that along the way they'll meet each other.
and friends rely on the same sun and rain
to meet their needs
as they grow together in their own ways.

created together

when you breathe
i will be in the warmth of your every breath.
when you see
i will be in your sight, looking back at you.
when you walk
i will be in your footsteps
and i will be walking towards you.
when you run your fingers through your hair
i will feel the strands.
when you laugh
i will be the life expanding in your chest.
and when you cry
i will be in the teardrops from your eyes.
when you smile
i will be in the curl of your lip
and in the twinkle in your eye.
when you sleep
i will be in your dreams.
and when you awake
i will be in the mirror when you look at yourself.
i will be so familiar
that when i appear in human form
you will think you've met me before
because i was created with you in the heavens.

door

it's easy to isolate yourself
in your home and feel languished
separated from everything in the world.
you are not disconnected
but only by a man-made door
and a belief that all is outside of you
and not knowing what is within you.
it is only when you open the door
and see the tree in front of your home
and smell the fresh air
that you awaken the world within you.
at all other times you are asleep
and nature is waiting for you to awaken
to see yourself.
you need to look outside at nature
to fully see what is within.

simple truth

the simple truth
about every human
is that they
want to love
and be loved.

bloom

we become
who we are supposed to be.
a rose bush is a rose bush
whether or not it has roses in bloom.
the roses will bloom in time
and so will you.

fully human

we exist by nature's design.
we are perfect in our perceived imperfections
fully human and complete
in illness, health, gratitude, anger, happiness, and sadness.
to think otherwise is to deny ourselves our nature and being.

center

as insignificant as you may feel
you are the center of your own universe.

the lake

as i found myself sitting by a lake
i found the lake also with me.
when i looked at my reflection in the lake
i saw the lake looking at me.

you are

you are beautiful
in your uncertainty and certainty
beyond your interior and exterior
and in what you share and don't share.
there is more to you than anyone will ever know.
you, yourself, will experience it
and know it better than anyone else.
people will catch parts of it.
and even though you are whole
you will never wholly give up
who you are.

silk

the things
that crush you
are turning everything
hard inside of
you into silk.

time

i do not work for time.
time works for me.
it holds me by my hand
when i am immersed in it.
it looks me in the eyes
and shows me where i was
and who i've become.
it unveils the future before me.
so do not worry and speculate; put your faith in time.
time tells all, but you also need to listen.
and the wise know that life is finite
and in that understanding, they seize time.

heartbeat

i carry on
holding my heart
listening to its song.
it beats.
it is music
attuned to the cosmos
as it hums to my soul
and stirs my life.
i dance.
i'm entranced
by the tune
of my heart.

i want

i want to be adorned with flowers
and be kissed by the sun.

i want to run through wild fields
and have the grass stain my feet green.

i want to sweat the morning dew
and have the moonlight grace my face at night.

i want to fall asleep to the hum of insects
and awaken to the melody of birds.

i want to shower in water falls
and sunbathe on the beach.

i want to fly with the butterflies
and dance with the wind.

i want to see the world through the eyes of a deer
and travel on the hooves of a horse.

i want to float to paradise in the ocean.
and sit with rocks by the sea.

i want the colors of autumn in my hair
and the perfume of spring on my skin.

i want the beauty of a misty mountain
and the depth of a canyon.

i want to be held by the branches of trees
and for their fruit to paint my lips sweet.

your melody

your laughter drives me crazy
there's nothing else
that tells a sweeter story.
since when have you been writing
such beautiful songs?
my languid heart has awakened
to your melody.

day or night

the sun peeks through the clouds
and shines down into your dark eyes.
i see two stars shining at me so bright
now i can't even remember
if it's day or night.

hidden leaf

are you some sort of thief?
have you found the hidden leaves?
one fell in your hair
i could've sworn it was from my tree.
you've always had a place on my branch
but i need to sit under the shade of your lashes.
in your eyes is where i find safety
i don't know of a better place to secure my vanity.
you see me standing at your front door
i'm going to step in.
the rain has begun to pour
and now you can close your eyes.
don't worry about being a host.
we already have strong ties.

i'll admit

i'll admit
i was looking for you
and i didn't see you coming
so i gave up
and you suddenly appeared.
i didn't know you'd be so near.

i'll admit
i loved you when i met you.
i didn't know that it was the tip
of the iceberg
and i was about to descend into love's sea
like a diver.

i'll admit
i felt you were out there
but worried
for you and me
that we'd never meet
but we were always linked
while i thought we were roaming free.

i'll admit
i felt lost before i met you.
i thought i was taking all the wrong turns
but i didn't know
i was on the right path
to find you.

i'll admit
before you
i was afraid of them all
but your light
drew me into safety
and all the dark fears faded away.

i'll admit
i was hurt
before i found you.
i thought my wounds
would be unsightly
but all you saw was my beauty.

i'll admit
i carried life's baggage
that i thought was too heavy
but you embraced it
and helped me unpack it.

i'll admit
at times i lived in darkness
but when i saw the sunrise
in your eyes
that was the beginning
of life's brightness.

i'll admit
i dreamt about you
what you'd look like
and how you'd feel
i didn't know
that you'd end up being real.

i'll admit
when we met
i had no idea what i was doing.
looking back i realized
it was all of love's doing.

i'll admit
it's been years now
since we've been together
but every day it still feels like
the first moment when i saw you
and yet like it's been forever.

he is

he is a truth
to my life and existence.
i can't describe why
i love him
i just know i love him.

shoes

i see you're running fast
and i look at you with envy.
you're getting ahead of me
and i look at myself with sadness.
i'm so far behind you.
perhaps you think you're better than me
but your shoes don't have the weight in them
that my shoes do.
and maybe someday i'll run as fast as you.
i need to get stronger
and overcome the weight.
when i gain the strength
to run faster in my shoes
perhaps i may even outrun you
because by then
you may have met a challenge
on your path that you've never seen
one that slows you down
and i already know how to get around
because i started running with
life's challenges in my shoes.

the hated

even the most hated
have been woven by the threads of love.
and their life hangs from love's thread.
after death
they are cleansed in love's bath.

ballerinas

it's almost a dream now,
but it was true.
i know because i held you.
and Life held onto you
but i wasn't sure
what Life meant to you anymore.
you were vibrant and became so frail.
i saw you were slipping away.
it was as if the grips of Life
were squeezing you out of Life's own hands.
your eyes spoke of yesterday
but they gazed into the future
like they were looking at an open space.
circumstances had held you hard
and you were hard in your ways
but i didn't know
you were also hard on your way.
perhaps your feet were on earth
but your mind was far away.
i understood that everyone wants a release
beyond any type of control
to just be lingering in the heavens
like a ballerina with wings.
and finally it came without any notice
the knock, which shook our lives
once it showed its face at our front door.
it must've been the one you had been waiting for.
and you walked out
between a blink and a heartbeat.
it seemed as though i had inhaled, a gasp

and you exhaled your last
giving away your breath
to the universe
or maybe to the next child
being born into this world.
and you sped away
like you had somewhere nicer to go.
it must've been a better deal.
i don't know.
but the hereafter beckoned you
as if it had prepared your final meal.
and i imagined you dancing around the stars
with winged ballerinas.

shattered

i shattered
into five thousand pieces.
i held those pieces in
as close as i could
and they came out
in five thousand tears.
as i looked in the mirror
the mirror shattered
into five thousand pieces
onto the floor
and i found five thousand fears
being swept
here and there.
and i just hoped
that some day
you would pick up those
five thousand pieces
and they'd become
five thousand pieces
of jewels in your hands.

flower bud

the flower bud said to the sky,
"i want to bloom
into a beautiful flower."
then the sky responded
to the flower bud,
"if you want to bloom
then i'm going to have to
both rain and shine
on you."

enlightened

i have found myself
becoming most enlightened
in my darkest
of times.
sometimes the darkness
cannot be extinguished
by anything
other than
your own light.

rise

i believe in you
the way i believe in the sun.
i know the sun will rise tomorrow
and so will you.

about him

the pens of the world
ran out of ink at the very suggestion
of me writing about him.
to write about him
would be to dive
into the deepest part of the ocean
to find the most brilliant pearl.
it would be to gaze
into the starry night
to answer the mysteries of the cosmos.
i will tell you that
he is the sun i orbit
and i am his universe.
we are the spectrum of colors
visible and invisible to the eye.
he is a continuum of me.
we are one, and to say who he is
is to say he is me.
i profess this in my capacity
as a witness to us.
he is not someone to write about
but to admire
in the mirror
of my heart.

originally

the child in you
reminds you
of who you
originally are.
playful.
wise.
curious.
adventurous.

reclaim

you'll be born pure
but the world will break you
and treat you
like there's something wrong with you
and like your brokenness is your fault.
don't believe the world.
don't believe the lies.
reclaim your life.
believe in your purity.
believe in the pieces
that create your own unique story
and make you whole.
your belief in your purity
will seal you together
once again.

confidence

confidence is without parameters.
it is developed over time.
confidence is knowing that circumstances do not define you.
it is knowing your spirit cannot be tainted or accessed.
confidence is knowing that it is okay to feel happy, shy, scared, nervous, anxious, surprised, and all your other emotions.
it is being okay with being fallible.
confidence is in seeing yourself for who you are and accepting yourself.
it is knowing that other people are equal to you despite their wit or wealth.
confidence is knowing that you can make your own decisions based on your own knowledge.
it is knowing that it is okay to not know something.
confidence is knowing that it is okay to ask questions.
it is developed when you go through many obstacles and you come out stronger.
confidence is developed by rising after falling and allowing yourself to fall again.
it is knowing you can look a person in the eye or choose to look away.
confidence is in stripping away all the false beliefs about yourself.
it is speaking the truth for the sake of truth and not for personal gain.
confidence is in taking control of defining your own life.
it is being able to laugh at yourself.
confidence is in embracing your total human nature.
it is you.
confidence is not outside of you, and only you can acquire it from within yourself.

oasis

in the desert of life
i found my oasis.
i found my love.

significance

when we observe the scale of this universal kingdom
we seem so infinitesimal.
yet even within ourselves we have trillions of cells
and each cell alone
even seems infinitesimal.
when we go down to the molecular level and then to the atomic level
we find that
we are a universe within the greater universe
and we are a lot larger
the deeper we go.
and we ask ourselves the question
how small or large are we?
finding our purpose
is what makes us feel
that we have some meaning.
is purpose something to be found
or is it already in our being?
now imagine this
the world is an infinite summation of things.
it needs those things to sustain itself.
imagine that you are one of those infinite things
and you are so significant
that the world would
cease to exist if you did not exist
during your appointed time in this universe.
you, all the way down to each atom
that creates you,
are a puzzle piece that fits,
perfectly to create the universe.
now ponder your significance and purpose.
you help form the universe.